Written by Odile Limousin
Illustrated by Beat Brüsch

Specialist Adviser:
Marlin A. Lovensheimer, Manager
Graphic Arts Services
Mead Paper

ISBN 0-944589-16-2
First U.S. Publication 1988 by
Young Discovery Library
217 Main St. • Ossining, NY 10562

©1985 by Editions Gallimard
Translated by Sarah Matthews
English text © 1986 by Moonlight Publishing Ltd.
Thanks to Aileen Buhl

The Story of Paper

What is paper made of?

YOUNG DISCOVERY LIBRARY

Paper is usually made from wood.

If you tear a sheet of paper,
you can see tiny fibers:
these are wood fibers.

What can you do with paper?

You can write on it, draw on it, fold it,
cut it. You can use it to make books,
newspapers, posters,
postcards, notebooks,
exercise books, and
a whole lot of other
things.

Can you recognize all the things
made of paper on these pages?

Paper? There are all kinds of paper for all sorts of uses. Very high quality, **rough** or **smooth**, for drawing or painting on; **fine** and **light** for writing on. It can be **absorbent**  as a sponge for lining a baby's diapers, or as **soft** as velvet for paper handkerchiefs.

It can act as a **filter,** holding all the tea leaves back while letting the flavor through from a tea bag. It can be **waterproofed**, so that liquids like yogurt, fruit juice, milk, do not run out of their cartons.

It can be **impossible to copy,** so that bank notes can't be forged, or **tough**, for wrapping and packing parcels.

Cardboard is made of paper too!

It is made by putting sheets of paper together in different ways.

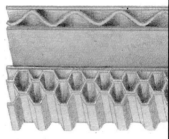

Cardboard is used for transporting anything fragile or heavy. It can be made so strong that it can be used to make briefcases, boxes, packing cases, even tables and chairs.

But be careful! Cardboard and paper catch fire easily.

Did people always have paper?

In prehistoric times people painted their pictures onto the walls of caves, using colors made from soil. Later, they wrote on things that could be kept for a long time such as bones, tree bark, shells, pottery. This meant ideas and stories could be passed on over the years.

Flint for engraving bone

In this workshop in Rome, they are engraving inscriptions onto stone, letter by letter. The Romans also used to write on tablets covered in wax. The wax could be smoothed over and used again and again.

Archaeologists have discovered vases, statues and tablets all covered in writing.

L·CAESARI
CLAVDIV
VI

The invention of parchment made it possible to make books.
In Asia Minor, the people of a city called Pergamon worked out the best way of drying calf, sheep, goat or deer skin. The skins were cleaned, scraped,

split, stretched, dried and polished with pumice stone. They ended up as beautifully smooth sheets, thin enough to handle easily, but thick enough for people to write on both sides without the ink soaking through.

In the Middle Ages, books and rolls of parchment were so precious that they were kept in libraries, chained to the shelves.

This is Egypt, 1800 years before the birth of Christ. A scribe, paintbrush in hand, is writing **hieroglyphics** on a long scroll made out of a special plant.

The special plant is called papyrus. It is a kind of reed which grows on the banks of the River Nile. The stalk was peeled and then cut into fine strips. Laid side by side and one over the other, the

strips were beaten flat and left to dry. The scibe's scroll would have been made by sticking several of these flat sheets together.

Papyrus gave us the word 'paper'.

Did you know that the oldest papermakers in the world are wasps?

These wasps make their nests in cardboard. They chew up bits of wood softened with saliva, and shape them into cells for their eggs. As they dry, they become strong and safe. It is said that a Chinese man, Tsai-Lun, watched the wasps, and invented paper by copying them. He crushed bamboo and mulberry wood, and made a liquid pulp. Then he filtered it and let it dry. **The first paper was made.** This happened in China, about 105 years after the birth of Jesus.

The pulp is shaken and sieved.

The crisscrossed fibers make a sheet of paper.

Paper traveled the world.

For over six hundred years, the Chinese kept their secret. Then, during a war, in 751, some Chinese papermakers were taken prisoner in Samarkand. From Samarkand the secret traveled to the Arabs, who improved the Chinese method by adding rags of hemp, cotton and linen. Soon the Khalifs, the kings of the Arab Empire, had the finest libraries of books in the world. They also used

paper to send messages from place to place on tiny slips fixed onto the legs of carrier pigeons.

In the Middle Ages, the Arabs who conquered Spain brought paper with them. Gradually the wonders of paper books were introduced to Europe. At first, merchants traded with the Arabs to buy shiploads of paper. Then the Europeans worked out a way of making paper for themselves. A whole new line of work grew up: not only papermakers, but also the ragmen who supplied them, traveling from village to village buying up old rags. They sold the rags to the paper mills, the first paper factories.

Ragman

Any old rags!
At the paper
mill, the rags
were sorted out.
All the stitches
and buttons were
taken out, then the

rags were left in the open until they
began to rot. After that they were cut
into strips and softened in a vat filled
with water. Hour after hour huge wooden
beaters would pound away at them,
breaking them into tiny bits. Mixed with
water, these tiny bits made a very runny
paper pulp. To make a better quality
pulp you added a little glue or resin.

The mill wheel
was turned by
the running water
of the river. As
it turned, it
worked the
heavy beaters.

The creation of a sheet of paper.

The workman plunges his mold — a rectangle with a very fine sieve in it — into a vat of paper pulp, then shakes the mold to make the pulp lie evenly. Once it has been drained, the sheet of paper is very damp and easily torn. It is carefully tipped onto a sheet of felt, then more felt is placed on top. Piles of these layers of paper and felt are put into a large press, which squeezes out nearly all the rest of the water. After that, the paper can be hung out on a line to finish drying.

You can see the sieve inside the mold. The metal shape makes the watermark.

If you hold the paper up to the light, you can see that the watermark shows up, because the paper is thinner at that point. Good quality paper has a watermark.

In the Middle Ages, books were rare and expensive, slowly written and painted by monks. Then, around 1450, Gutenberg invented  a way of printing, using small letters on

  the end of little metal bars, and a special printing press.

Now several copies of a book could be made quickly and easily.

There were more and more readers, but the papermakers found themselves running short of rags for their paper. In the eighteenth century a French scientist called Réaumur observed the paper wasps building their nests out of wood, as the Chinese had done before, and suggested making paper from wood. Paper is made from wood to this day.

The printer puts the letters together to make the text, rubs ink over them and presses a sheet of paper onto them to make a copy.

Nowadays whole forests are cut down to make the millions of tons of paper we use every day. The trees are felled and then floated downriver, or carried on trucks to the paper factories.

Pine saplings

How can we make sure we don't have a planet without trees?

As soon as they are cut down, the trees are replaced with saplings. But trees don't grow overnight. A beech takes over sixty years to mature. A pine tree takes only twenty years. That is why so many forests are planted with pine trees nowadays.

| Pine | Fir | Birch | Poplar |

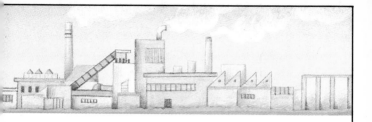

**It took nearly
one pound of wood
to make this book
you are reading!**

Old papers packed
for recycling

Scientists are working all
the time to try and find
ways of making paper out
of plants like hemp and
esparto grass. At the same time, to
avoid waste, papermakers are using old
paper. Once it has been de-inked and
recycled, a ton of old paper can save
the lives of eight trees.

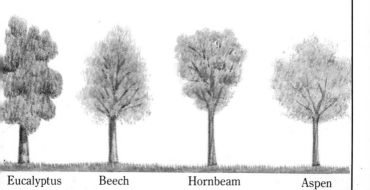

Eucalyptus   Beech   Hornbeam   Aspen

Look at the paper a newspaper is made of: it's greyish, and if you write on it, the ink spreads. Newsprint, as this kind of paper is called, is made of **mechanical pulp**: logs are stripped, ground up, and broken down into tiny bits which soften as they are soaked in water.

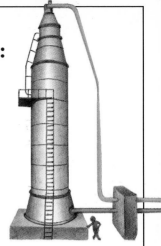

A boiler for chemical pulp

The pages in a note book are smooth and white, your pen slides over them. This paper has been made from **chemical pulp.** The wood shavings have been boiled at very high temperatures in a special boiler before being made into paper.

Making mechanical pulp

In the paper factory

Machines do the work that the old paper mills used to do. But instead of making paper a sheet at a time, now they make huge rolls of it, turning out 600 yards a minute — that's six times as long as a football field.

The machine is worked by computer.
1. The pulp is poured onto a wire mesh which moves along like a conveyor belt.

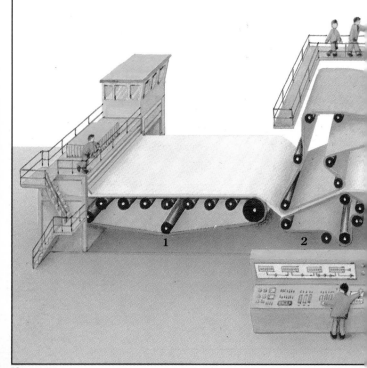

2. The damp pulp is moved onto rollers — it has now become a sheet of paper.

3. The paper receives its watermark as it is pressed between the rollers.

4. Heated cylinders dry the paper as it passes through.

5. Sometimes rollers are used to make it smooth and shiny.

6. The paper is rolled up ready to be used by the printer.

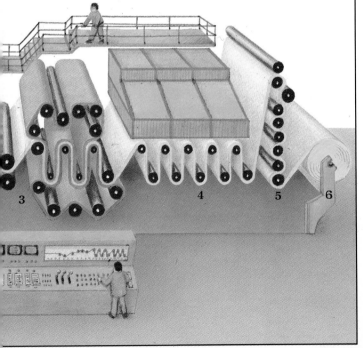

Old newspaper　　　　Bowls　　　　Wallpaper paste

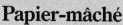

Papier-mâché

Tear old newspapers into thin strips. Leave them to soak overnight in a bowl of warm water. Next day pour 4 cupfuls of water into a bowl, and mix in a soupspoonful of the wallpaper paste. Take handfuls of the soaked paper, squeeze out the water, and knead in some of the wallpaper paste to make a smooth pulp.

You can use pastry tins as molds.

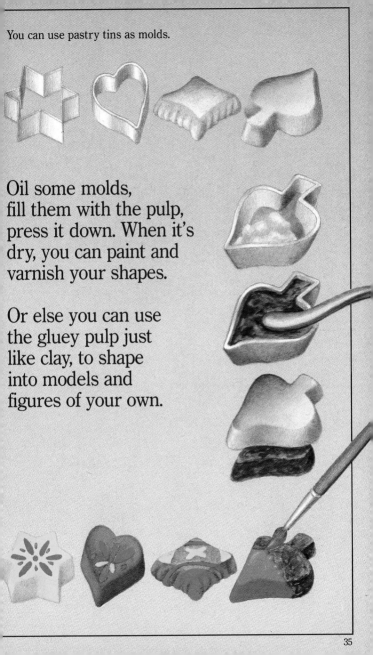

Oil some molds,
fill them with the pulp,
press it down. When it's
dry, you can paint and
varnish your shapes.

Or else you can use
the gluey pulp just
like clay, to shape
into models and
figures of your own.

Did you hear these words today?

paperback

paperboy/papergirl

paper chase

paper clip

paper cutter

paper doll

paperhanger

paper knife

papier-mâché

paper profit

paper thin

paper tiger

paper-train

paperweight

Index